DIARIES AND AUTOBIOGRAPHIES
THROUGHOUT AMERICAN HISTORY

NARRATIVE

OF THE

LIFE

OF

FREDERICK DOUGLASS,

AN

AMERICAN SLAVE.

WRITTEN BY HIMSELF.

BOSTON:

PUBLISHED AT THE ANTI-SLAVERY OFFICE

BY ABBY BADACH DOYLE

Gareth Stevens
PUBLISHING

Please visit our website, www.garethstevens.com. For a free color catalog of all our high-quality books, call toll free 1-800-542-2595 or fax 1-877-542-2596.

Library of Congress Cataloging-in-Publication Data

Names: Doyle, Abby Badach, author.
Title: Diaries and autobiographies / Abby Badach Doyle.
Description: New York : Gareth Stevens Publishing, [2020] | Series: Journey to the past: investigating primary sources | Includes index.
Identifiers: LCCN 2018059666| ISBN 9781538240342 (pbk.) | ISBN 9781538240366 (library bound) | ISBN 9781538240359 (6 pack)
Subjects: LCSH: Autobiographies--United States--Juvenile literature. | American diaries--Juvenile literature. | United States--History--Sources--Juvenile literature. | United States--Biography--Juvenile literature.
Classification: LCC CT25 .D69 2020 | DDC 920--dc23
LC record available at https://lccn.loc.gov/2018059666

First Edition

Published in 2020 by
Gareth Stevens Publishing
111 East 14th Street, Suite 349
New York, NY 10003

Designer: Katelyn E. Reynolds
Editor: Jill Keppeler

Photo credits: Cover, pp. 1, 13 (inset) http://docsouth.unc.edu/neh/douglass/ douglass.html/Quadell/Wikipedia.org; cover, pp. 1-32 (wood background) Miro Novak/ Shutterstock.com; cover, pp. 1-32 (old paper) Andrey_Kuzmin/Shutterstock.com; p. 5 FotoDuets/Shutterstock.com; p. 7 (main) GraphicaArtis/Getty Images; p. 7 (inset) Archiving Early America (http://www.earlyamerica.com/lives/franklin/). Bryan/ Lupo/Wikipedia.org; p. 9 (map) MPI/Getty Images; pp. 9 (inset), 13 (main), 15 (inset), 17, 19, 21 (main), 25 courtesy of the Library of Congress; p. 10 VT750/Shutterstock.com; p. 11 Tungsten/Wikipedia.org; p. 14 Carol M. Highsmith/Buyenlarge/Getty Images; p. 15 (main) Scan of an old book, originally from this Reddit post (https://www.reddit.com/ r/books/comments/gp2e7/before_i_sold_this_i_thought_you_all_might_like/)./ Delirium/Wikipedia.org; p. 21 (inset) Jeff Greenberg/UIG via Getty Images; p. 23 Honoring a Legend (https://www.flickr.com/photos/marine_corps/13870772273/)/ Jasonanaggie/Wikipedia.org; p. 27 (main) Malcolm Ali/WireImage/Getty Images; p. 27 (inset) Astrid Stawiarz/Getty Images; p. 29 courtesy of NASA.

Printed in the United States of America

CPSIA compliance information: Batch #CS19GS: For further information contact Gareth Stevens, New York, New York at 1-800-542-2595.

CONTENTS

WORDS IN THE GLOSSARY APPEAR IN BOLD TYPE THE FIRST TIME THEY ARE USED IN THE TEXT.

WHAT'S THE
DIFFERENCE?

Primary sources are firsthand sources of information. They're like puzzle pieces! Each one shows a bit of the bigger picture of what life was like at the time it was created. In diaries and autobiographies, writers capture how they felt about what happened.

In some ways, a diary is like a trusted friend. In a diary, you can share your thoughts and feelings . . . or even your biggest secrets! When keeping a diary, the writer might not think anyone will ever see it. However, an autobiography is a history of a person's life written by that person. It's usually meant to be published. The author writes it to share their story with the world. Both types of sources can get you up close with history.

ANALYZE IT!

DO YOU KEEP A DIARY? PRETEND YOU'RE SOMEONE READING IT 200 YEARS FROM NOW. WHAT DOES YOUR DIARY REVEAL ABOUT LIVING IN TODAY'S TIME PERIOD?

READ LIKE
A HISTORIAN

DIARIES AND AUTOBIOGRAPHIES SHOW THE WRITER'S THOUGHTS AND FEELINGS ABOUT IMPORTANT EVENTS. THAT MAKES THEM MORE PERSONAL THAN A TEXTBOOK. HOWEVER, A GOOD HISTORIAN CHECKS THE FACTS. A DIARY OR AUTOBIOGRAPHY MIGHT REFLECT THE WRITER'S **BIASES**. WHEN READING, REMEMBER TO CONSIDER OTHER POINTS OF VIEW. THERE ARE ALWAYS MANY SIDES TO THE SAME STORY!

WHEN WRITING AN AUTOBIOGRAPHY, THE AUTHOR MIGHT START FROM SCRATCH OR TURN TO EARLIER WRITINGS (SUCH AS A DIARY) FOR INSPIRATION.

BENJAMIN FRANKLIN

Benjamin Franklin, one of the Founding Fathers of the United States, lived a long, interesting life. He wrote one of the first (and most famous) examples of an American autobiography. Franklin was a writer, publisher, scientist, inventor, and politician. He had a lot of stories to tell.

At age 11, he invented swim fins. At age 25, he started the nation's first lending library. At age 45, he helped start the nation's first public hospital. He didn't start writing his autobiography until he was 65 years old . . . maybe because he was too busy before then! He told stories about many of these events in his autobiography. Franklin wrote for much of his life. He also helped write the Declaration of Independence.

ANALYZE IT!

BENJAMIN FRANKLIN PUBLISHED A LOT OF WRITING IN HIS LIFETIME. WHY DO YOU THINK HE DECIDED TO WRITE AN AUTOBIOGRAPHY?

ONE WRITER, MANY NAMES

AS A TEENAGER, BENJAMIN FRANKLIN FOUND A SNEAKY WAY TO WRITE FOR HIS BROTHER'S NEWSPAPER. HE WROTE LETTERS AS "SILENCE DOGOOD" AND SLIPPED THEM UNDER THE PRINT SHOP DOOR AT NIGHT. READERS LOVED THEM! AS AN ADULT, FRANKLIN PUBLISHED *POOR RICHARD'S ALMANACK* AS "RICHARD SAUNDERS." IT INCLUDED WEATHER REPORTS, RECIPES, AND WITTY SAYINGS.

FRANKLIN'S AUTOBIOGRAPHY

PRIVATE LIFE

OF THE LATE

BENJAMIN FRANKLIN, LL.D.

LATE MINISTER PLENIPOTENTIARY FROM THE UNITED
STATES OF AMERICA TO FRANCE, &c. &c. &c.

Originally written by Himself,
AND NOW TRANSLATED FROM THE FRENCH.

TO WHICH ARE ADDED,

SOME ACCOUNT OF HIS PUBLIC LIFE, A VARIETY OF
ANECDOTES CONCERNING HIM, BY M. M. BRISSOT,
CONDORCET, ROCHEFOUCAULT, LE ROY, &c. &c.

AND THE EULOGIUM OF M. FAUCHET,
CONSTITUTIONAL BISHOP OF THE DEPARTMENT OF CALVADOS,
AND A MEMBER OF THE NATIONAL CONVENTION.

Eripuit cœlo fulmen, mox sceptra tyrannis. Turgot.
A Paris, ce grand homme, dans votre ancien régime, seroit resté dans l'ob-
scurité ; comment employer le fils d'un chandelier ? Le Roy.

LONDON:
PRINTED FOR J. PARSONS, NO. 21, PATER-NOSTER ROW.
1793.

BENJAMIN FRANKLIN DIDN'T WRITE HIS AUTOBIOGRAPHY ALL AT ONCE. HE STARTED WITH THE FIRST (AND LONGEST) SECTION ABOUT HIS YOUNGER YEARS. TEN YEARS LATER, HE WROTE THE REST.

JOURNALS OF LEWIS AND CLARK

Have you ever traveled far away to visit a new place? Things can be very unfamiliar. The plants and animals you see and the languages you hear might all seem strange to you. Even the air might smell different! Those kinds of details are exactly what Meriwether Lewis and William Clark wrote about when they explored the American West.

In 1804, President Thomas Jefferson sent Lewis and Clark on a cross-country journey to explore the new land in the Louisiana Purchase. Their writing was careful and scientific. They drew detailed maps and sketches. They documented, or created a record of, patterns in weather, geology, and biology. As the first accounts of this region, their diaries are important primary sources. Together, the notebooks contain more than a million words.

ANALYZE IT!

IF YOU KNEW THE PRESIDENT OF THE UNITED STATES PLANNED TO READ YOUR JOURNAL, WOULD YOU WRITE DIFFERENTLY THAN IF IT WOULD BE KEPT PRIVATE?

THE PATH OF
THE EXPEDITION

LEWIS AND CLARK'S JOURNEY BEGAN IN SAINT LOUIS, MISSOURI, IN MAY 1804. FOR THE NEXT 18 MONTHS, THEY TRAVELED NORTHWEST OVER RIVERS, PLAINS, AND MOUNTAINS. THEY REACHED MODERN-DAY OREGON IN NOVEMBER 1805 AND STAYED THE WINTER AT FORT CLATSOP, NOW A NATIONAL HISTORICAL PARK. THEY HEADED HOME THE FOLLOWING SPRING.

MAP SHOWING THE LOUISIANA PURCHASE COMPARED TO THE CURRENT UNITED STATES

JOURNAL ENTRY

WHERE DOES YOUR EYE GO FIRST?

WILLIAM CLARK WROTE THIS ENTRY.
WHAT DO YOU THINK OF HIS WRITING?

WHAT CAN THIS SKETCH TELL YOU ABOUT
CLARK'S TRAINING AS A MAP MAKER?

WHY WERE DRAWINGS LIKE THIS
SO IMPORTANT TO THE MISSION?

WHO IS THE INTENDED AUDIENCE
FOR THIS DRAWING?

IN THE JOURNAL ENTRY ABOVE RIGHT, DATED JULY 2, 1805, WILLIAM CLARK DREW A MAP OF THE GREAT FALLS OF THE MISSOURI RIVER.

Lewis and Clark didn't write in one big journal. Their journals are made up of a collection of different notebooks, field notes, and scraps of paper. Since the explorers kept so many different notebooks and pages, some historians wonder if we have them all. A few of their journals were discovered in unexpected places more than 100 years later!

The explorers didn't write every day. Lewis and Clark wrote most of the entries, but other men from their group, the Corps of Discovery, contributed too. Some notebooks are surprisingly neat and tidy. That makes some historians wonder if they were really written during the expedition or after the men returned. However, some evidence suggests that the explorers kept their journals in a tin box to protect them from the elements.

SIGN FOR THE LEWIS AND CLARK NATIONAL HISTORIC TRAIL

SACAGAWEA:
A HISTORY MYSTERY

THE EXPLORERS HAD HELP FROM MANY NATIVE AMERICANS, INCLUDING THE LEGENDARY SACAGAWEA. YOU'VE PROBABLY HEARD HER STORY, BUT SHE NEVER KEPT A JOURNAL. THE ONLY WAY WE KNOW HER IS THROUGH LEWIS AND CLARK'S EYES. IMAGINE HOW SHE FELT WHEN SHE LEARNED SHE WOULD BE TRAVELING WITH THEM. WAS SHE EXCITED, FRIGHTENED, OR BOTH?

LEWIS AND CLARK WERE BRAVE EXPLORERS—BUT THEY WERE BAD SPELLERS. FOR EXAMPLE, THEIR JOURNALS INCLUDE AT LEAST 15 DIFFERENT SPELLINGS OF THE WORD "MOSQUITO!"

FREDERICK DOUGLASS

Imagine that you worked hard to accomplish something **significant,** but people spread rumors that you didn't actually do it. How would that make you feel? That's what happened to Frederick Douglass. Until age 20, he endured **brutal** treatment as a slave in Maryland. He escaped by disguising himself as a free black sailor. Afterward, he began speaking out to share his story. Still, some people said he was lying!

Douglass published his first autobiography, *Narrative of the Life of Frederick Douglass*, in 1845. He included names of specific places and people from his enslavement to prove the facts. It was a brave decision: even though he had escaped, Douglass was still legally a slave. At any time, he could have been captured and re-enslaved.

ANALYZE IT!

FREDERICK DOUGLASS PUBLISHED HIS AUTOBIOGRAPHY DESPITE THE RISK OF BEING RECAPTURED. WHY DO YOU THINK HE WAS WILLING TO TAKE THE CHANCE?

LEARNING TO READ

IN MANY PLACES, IT WAS A CRIME TO TEACH A SLAVE TO READ AND WRITE. AS A CHILD, FREDERICK DOUGLASS LEARNED THE ALPHABET IN SECRET FROM HIS MASTER'S WIFE. HE TRADED SCRAPS OF BREAD FOR READING LESSONS FROM NEIGHBORHOOD CHILDREN. DOUGLASS BELIEVED THAT KNOWLEDGE AND EDUCATION ARE FUNDAMENTAL TO FREEDOM.

FREDERICK'S AUTOBIOGRAPHY

NARRATIVE

OF THE

LIFE

OF

FREDERICK DOUGLASS,

AN

AMERICAN SLAVE.

WRITTEN BY HIMSELF.

BOSTON:
PUBLISHED AT THE ANTI-SLAVERY OFFICE,
No. 25 CORNHILL
1845.

AFTER HIS BOOK WAS PUBLISHED, DOUGLASS TRAVELED TO EUROPE TO AVOID BEING CAPTURED. HIS FRIENDS IN ENGLAND PURCHASED HIS FREEDOM IN 1847.

After Douglass published his first book, his public work was just getting started. He traveled and wrote often to promote racial equality. He helped other slaves escape on the Underground Railroad. He met with President Abraham Lincoln to **advocate** for equal pay for black soldiers. Eventually, he went on to work in Washington, DC, under five different presidents.

Douglass wrote three autobiographies. His second book, *My Bondage and My Freedom*, was published in 1855. It expanded on his first book with more detail about his early life and escape. His third and final autobiography, *Life and Times of Frederick Douglass*, was published when Douglass was 63 years old. His final book examined his life's work, the nation's progress, and the work yet to be done.

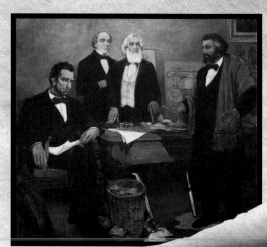

**DOUGLASS MEETING WITH
PRESIDENT ABRAHAM LINCOLN**

OTHER SLAVE NARRATIVES

SLAVE **MEMOIRS** ARE IMPORTANT PRIMARY SOURCES TO UNDERSTAND THE TRUE CRUELTY OF SLAVERY. OTHER NOTABLE AUTOBIOGRAPHIES INCLUDE BOOKER T. WASHINGTON'S *UP FROM SLAVERY* AND ELIZABETH KECKLEY'S *BEHIND THE SCENES; OR, THIRTY YEARS A SLAVE AND FOUR YEARS IN THE WHITE HOUSE.* (SHE LATER BECAME MARY TODD LINCOLN'S DRESSMAKER AND FRIEND!)

UP FROM SLAVERY
AN AUTOBIOGRAPHY
BOOKER T. WASHINGTON

BOOKER T. WASHINGTON

BOOKER T. WASHINGTON WAS BORN INTO SLAVERY IN 1856. IN 1901, PRESIDENT THEODORE ROOSEVELT INVITED HIM TO DINNER AT THE WHITE HOUSE. THIS WAS A SURPRISE AND A REALLY BIG DEAL AT THE TIME!

EMILY QUINER,
CIVIL WAR NURSE

Emily Quiner lived a pretty common life for a woman of her time. She worked at the family newspaper in Wisconsin. She attended church. She liked to play chess, sing, and sew. She became a teacher. However, Quiner's diary made this typical midwestern woman a distinctive voice in Civil War history!

Quiner started her diary in April 1861, when the American Civil War began. Two years later, at age 23, Quiner volunteered at a Union hospital with her sister Fannie. Together, they traveled to Memphis, Tennessee, to care for sick and wounded soldiers. Quiner's diary offers a deeply personal look at conditions in the hospital and the soldiers' suffering. Modern Civil War scholars have used her diary entries as an important primary source.

ANALYZE IT!

WITH THE EXCEPTION OF HER SISTER, EMILY QUINER'S FAMILY AND FRIENDS UP NORTH DIDN'T SEE THE EFFECTS OF WAR FIRSTHAND. WHAT DO YOU THINK SHE WANTED THEM TO KNOW?

MEDICINE
IN THE CIVIL WAR

CIVIL WAR DOCTORS KNEW THAT A CLEAN HOSPITAL KEPT
SOLDIERS HEALTHY. HOWEVER, THEY DIDN'T HAVE MODERN CLEANING
OR ANTIBACTERIAL PRODUCTS. MANY CIVIL WAR FIELD HOSPITALS WERE
SET UP QUICKLY. THEY WERE OVERCROWDED AND DIRTY. IN FACT, MORE
SOLDIERS DIED DURING THE WAR FROM INFECTION AND DISEASE THAN
DURING BATTLE ITSELF.

MANY COMMON MEDICAL TREATMENTS OF TODAY
DIDN'T EXIST AT THE TIME OF THE CIVIL WAR.
CONDITIONS IN HOSPITALS COULD BE VERY ROUGH.

JOHN MUIR, FATHER OF OUR NATIONAL PARKS

John Muir was an explorer, writer, and one of America's most influential **conservationists.** He kept detailed journals and drew sketches of his adventures in the American West. He traveled from the Sierra Nevada Mountains in California to the glaciers of Alaska. Muir's writing appeared in newspapers all over the country, from California to New York. Some of his journals later became books. His poetic and persuasive writing inspired common people and lawmakers to step up and do something to protect the **environment.**

In 1892, Muir established the Sierra Club, which still exists today to protect the wilderness. Through the years, Muir's writings and meetings with influential people helped inspire the creation of many national parks, including Yosemite, Sequoia, and the Grand Canyon.

ANALYZE IT!

UNLIKE LEWIS AND CLARK, MUIR OFTEN TRAVELED BY HIMSELF. WHY WAS IT ESPECIALLY IMPORTANT FOR HIM TO KEEP A JOURNAL?

AMERICA'S MOST EPIC CAMPING TRIP

IN MAY 1903, PRESIDENT THEODORE ROOSEVELT MET JOHN MUIR FOR AN **EPIC** FOUR-DAY ADVENTURE. THEY RODE HORSES, HIKED, AND CAMPED IN THE CHILLY MOUNTAIN AIR. THE TRIP INSPIRED ROOSEVELT TO PRESERVE THE WILDERNESS FOR FUTURE GENERATIONS. HE STARTED THE US FOREST SERVICE AND SET ASIDE 230 MILLION ACRES FOR NATIONAL MONUMENTS, PARKS, AND WILDLIFE PRESERVES.

PRESIDENT THEODORE ROOSEVELT

JOHN MUIR

PRESIDENT THEODORE ROOSEVELT'S CAMPING TRIP WITH JOHN MUIR INSPIRED HIS REPUTATION AS "THE CONSERVATIONIST PRESIDENT."

HELEN KELLER

Helen Keller's autobiography is an American classic. She overcame many obstacles in her life with courage. When she was 19 months old, an illness left her deaf and blind. As a child, she was wild and had a hot temper. At age 6, she met Anne Sullivan, a patient teacher who helped her understand words and language.

Keller wrote and published her autobiography, *The Story of My Life*, in 1903. For a deaf and blind person, it was a big challenge! She wrote first using a Braille machine and then a traditional typewriter. She could read back the Braille parts to edit them, but the typewritten words required an extra step. A friend who could see would have to read what she typed, then translate it back by signing into Keller's hands.

ANALYZE IT!

THINK ABOUT THE OBSTACLES HELEN KELLER HAD TO OVERCOME. WHY IS THE QUALITY OF HER AUTOBIOGRAPHY JUST AS IMPORTANT AS ITS CONTENT?

HOW CAN THE BLIND READ?

BRAILLE, INVENTED IN 1824, IS A SYSTEM OF RAISED DOTS READ BY MOVING ONE'S FINGERS OVER THEM. EACH COMBINATION REPRESENTS A LETTER, **PUNCTUATION** MARK, OR SPACE. TODAY, BRAILLE IS STILL IMPORTANT, BUT THERE ARE OTHER OPTIONS. SCREEN READERS, AUDIOBOOKS, AND SPECIAL APPS HELP BLIND PEOPLE BY READING PRINTED WORDS OUT LOUD.

KELLER'S AUTOBIOGRAPHY

THE STORY OF MY LIFE
HELEN KELLER

Mr. William Gibson wrote
The Miracle Worker from
this book. Mr. Gibson donated
it to the home on May 26, 2000

KELLER'S AUTOBIOGRAPHY HAS BEEN PUBLISHED IN MORE THAN 50 LANGUAGES AND HAS REMAINED IN PRINT FOR MORE THAN 100 YEARS.

CHESTER NEZ, NAVAJO CODE TALKER

In the 1930s, many Navajo children were forbidden from speaking their native language at school. In his memoir, *Code Talker*, Chester Nez wrote about the harsh punishments they'd receive for doing so. Students caught speaking Navajo would have their mouths washed out with bitter soap. Sometimes, they would even get a beating. Less than 15 years later, Nez used that same Navajo language as a secret weapon for the United States in World War II.

The Navajo code talkers helped US forces transmit messages during battle in a language the enemy couldn't understand. Communicating in code could be **stressful**. Many times, it made the difference between life and death. Nez's autobiography is an inspiring story about courage, sacrifice, and loyalty to both one's **heritage** and country.

ANALYZE IT!

OF THE 29 ORIGINAL NAVAJO CODE TALKERS, CHESTER NEZ WAS THE ONLY ONE TO WRITE AN AUTOBIOGRAPHY. WHAT CAN HIS **PERSPECTIVE** TELL US?

CRACKING THE CODE

THE NAVAJO LANGUAGE MADE A SECURE AND FAST CODE. TO SPELL WORDS, CODE TALKERS USED A LIST OF 26 NAVAJO WORDS THAT STOOD FOR ENGLISH LETTERS. OTHER TIMES, NAVAJOS WOULD TRANSLATE THE WHOLE SENTENCE. FOR MILITARY VOCABULARY WITHOUT A NAVAJO WORD, THEY WOULD PICK A SIMILAR TERM INSPIRED BY NATURE. FOR EXAMPLE, "BATTLESHIP" WAS *LO-TSO* (WHALE).

PEOPLE DON'T ALWAYS WRITE AUTOBIOGRAPHIES ALL BY THEMSELVES. CHESTER NEZ WROTE HIS WITH THE HELP OF A COAUTHOR, JUDITH SCHIESS AVILA.

LYNN GOLDSMITH,
CIVIL RIGHTS
ACTIVIST

In the 1950s and 1960s, Jim Crow laws separated black and white people in schools, public transportation, and even bathrooms. Civil rights leaders such as Martin Luther King Jr. rallied people to fight for equal rights. Many activists practiced nonviolence, including civil disobedience and peaceful protests.

Lynn Goldsmith, a college freshman from Massachusetts, was one of those volunteers. In the summer of 1965, she kept a detailed diary when she traveled to South Carolina to help people register to vote. Her words show the bravery and passion shared by many young activists of the time. Goldsmith also wrote about some scary experiences. At a march, she was picked up and thrown by police. Then, she was arrested and sent to a dirty jail cell. Her journals capture history in a personal way.

ANALYZE IT!

WHAT ELSE WAS HAPPENING IN THE CIVIL RIGHTS MOVEMENT AT THE TIME LYNN GOLDSMITH WAS WRITING HER JOURNALS? WHAT HADN'T HAPPENED YET?

MUSIC AND
THE CIVIL RIGHTS MOVEMENT

MANY CIVIL RIGHTS-RELATED SONGS WERE FROM THE AFRICAN AMERICAN SPIRITUAL, GOSPEL, AND FOLK MUSIC TRADITIONS. CIVIL RIGHTS ACTIVISTS HAD A SONG TO MATCH ANY MOOD. SOMETIMES, THEY SANG JOYFUL SONGS TO KEEP SPIRITS UP DURING TENSE MOMENTS OR LONG MARCHES. OTHER TIMES, THEY SANG SOFTLY JUST TO PASS THE TIME.

CIVIL RIGHTS ACTIVISTS OFTEN CARRIED SIGNS WHEN THEY MARCHED AND PROTESTED.

PRESIDENT BARACK OBAMA

Many, but not all, US presidents have written autobiographies. Some write about their childhoods and early lives. Others write about their time in the Oval Office or after the presidency. Some presidents have written multiple autobiographies.

President Barack Obama, the 44th US president, was the first African American to hold the office. In *Dreams from My Father*, published in 1995, Obama wrote about growing up in Hawaii and Indonesia. His parents divorced when he was 2 years old. He barely knew his father and was raised mostly by his mother and grandparents. Obama published his second autobiography in October 2006, while he was serving as a US senator from Illinois. The **Audacity** of Hope focuses more on his political views. Obama announced his plan to run for president shortly after its release.

ANALYZE IT!

NOT EVERYONE AGREES WITH THE DECISIONS MADE BY A US PRESIDENT. DO YOU THINK PRESIDENTS WRITE THEIR AUTOBIOGRAPHIES FOR THEIR FANS, THEIR CRITICS, OR BOTH? WHY?

AUTOBIOGRAPHIES OF FIRST LADIES

THE AUTOBIOGRAPHIES OF PRESIDENTS' WIVES OFFER A UNIQUE PERSPECTIVE ON MARRIAGE AND FAMILY LIFE. MANY SHARE DEEPLY PERSONAL STORIES. IN HER 1994 MEMOIR, BARBARA BUSH (WIFE OF GEORGE H. W. BUSH) SHARED ABOUT LOSING HER 3-YEAR-OLD DAUGHTER TO CANCER. IN MICHELLE OBAMA'S 2018 AUTOBIOGRAPHY, *BECOMING*, SHE WROTE ABOUT DEALING WITH RACISM.

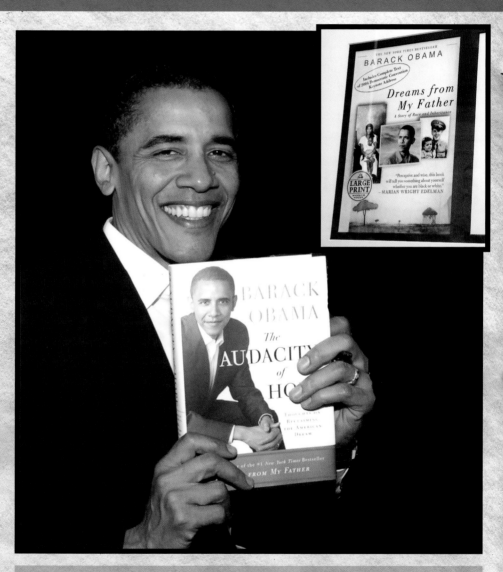

FOR MANY US PRESIDENTS, WRITING AN AUTOBIOGRAPHY IS A WAY TO PRESERVE THEIR PERSPECTIVE.

JOURNALS FROM SPACE!

Peggy Whitson's career has been out of this world. This record-breaking NASA astronaut took part in three missions on the International Space Station, completed 10 spacewalks, and spent a total of 665 days in space—more than any other US astronaut to date.

During her training and spaceflights, Whitson posted frequently to social media sites Twitter and Tumblr. She kept online journals, published on NASA's website, with details about what life is really like in outer space. She wrote about staying in shape, what a lift-off feels like, and, of course, what astronauts eat. (Spoiler alert: The food is tasteless and dry, but a little ketchup goes a long way!) Whitson's journals introduced a new generation to the mystery and wonder of space travel. She retired in June 2018.

ANALYZE IT!

WHAT SURPRISES YOU ABOUT PEGGY WHITSON'S POSTS FROM SPACE? WHAT ARE YOU STILL CURIOUS TO KNOW ABOUT LIFE AS AN ASTRONAUT?

WHAT'S NEXT?
DIARIES IN THE DIGITAL AGE

IN BENJAMIN FRANKLIN'S TIME, IT TOOK WEEKS FOR A SHIP TO TRANSPORT A LETTER FROM THE UNITED STATES TO ENGLAND. TODAY, IT TAKES SECONDS TO POST TO THE INTERNET! BLOGS, SOCIAL MEDIA, VIDEOS, AND PODCASTS CAPTURE HISTORY IN REAL TIME. EVEN SO, SOME PEOPLE STILL PREFER TO WRITE WITH PAPER AND PEN. HOW ABOUT YOU?

PEGGY WHITSON IS @ASTROPEGGY ON TWITTER.
YOU CAN STILL SEE MANY OF HER TWEETS FROM SPACE THERE.

GLOSSARY

accuracy: freedom from mistakes

advocate: to support or speak in favor of something

audacity: a willingness to take bold risks

bias: a belief that some people or ideas are better than others

brutal: especially violent or severe

conservationist: a person concerned with conservation, or the care of nature

environment: the conditions that surround a living thing and affect the way it lives; the natural world in which a plant or animal lives

epic: very great, large, or impressive

heritage: something that comes from past members of a family or group

memoir: a written account in which someone describes past experiences

perspective: point of view

punctuation: the marks, such as periods (.) and commas (,), that are used to make the meaning of a piece of writing clear

significant: large enough to be noticed or have an effect; very important

stressful: full of or causing stress, or a feeling of worry

FOR MORE INFORMATION

BOOKS

Shea, Nicole. *Frederick Douglass in His Own Words*. New York, New York: Gareth Stevens Publishing, 2014.

Kennon, Caroline. *Hellen Keller in Her Own Words*. New York, New York: Gareth Stevens Publishing, 2015.

McKinney, Devon. *The Lewis and Clark Expedition: The Corps of Discovery*. New York, New York: PowerKids Press, 2017.

WEBSITES

The Electric Ben Franklin
ushistory.org/franklin
The Independence Hall Association offers fun facts and interactive activities about this Founding Father.

Lewis and Clark's Expedition
kids.nationalgeographic.com/explore/history/lewis-and-clark/
Learn more about the journey of Lewis and Clark with stories, pictures, and maps.

Peggy Whitson Videos
nasa.gov/astronauts/biographies/peggy-a-whitson/videos
Watch clips of Peggy Whitson on NASA space shuttle launches, spacewalks, and more.

INDEX